Purpose Inspired:
Reflections on Conscious Living
VOLUME 5

By Wayne Visser

Paperback edition published in 2022
by Kaleidoscope Futures, Narborough, UK.

Copyright © 2022 Wayne Visser.

All rights reserved. No part of this publication may be reproduced, stored in a retrieval system, or transmitted, in any form or by any means, electronic, mechanical, photocopying, recording or otherwise, except as permitted by the UK Copyright, Designs and Patents Act 1988, without the prior permission of the publisher.

Cover photography and design by Wayne Visser.

Printing and distribution by Lulu.com.

ISBN 978-1-908875-52-5

Non-fiction Books by Wayne Visser

Beyond Reasonable Greed: Why Sustainable Business is a Much Better Idea!

South Africa: Reasons to Believe

Corporate Citizenship in Africa: Lessons from the Past, Paths to the Future

Business Frontiers: Social Responsibility, Sustainable Development and Economic Justice

The A to Z of Corporate Social Responsibility: A Complete Reference Guide to Concepts, Codes and Organisations

Making A Difference: Purpose-Inspired Leadership for Corporate Sustainability & Responsibility

Landmarks for Sustainability

The Top 50 Sustainability Books

The World Guide to CSR: A Country by Country Analysis of Corporate Sustainability and Responsibility

The Age of Responsibility: CSR 2.0 and the New DNA of Business

- The Quest for Sustainable Business: An Epic Journey in Search of Corporate Responsibility
- Corporate Sustainability & Responsibility: An Introductory Text on CSR Theory & Practice – Past, Present & Future
- CSR 2.0: Transforming Corporate Sustainability and Responsibility
- Disrupting the Future: Great Ideas for Creating a Much Better World
- This is Tomorrow: Artists for a Sustainable Future
- Sustainable Frontiers: Unlocking Change Through Business, Leadership and Innovation
- The CSR International Research Compendium: Volumes 1-3
- The World Guide to Sustainable Enterprise: Volumes 1-4
- The Little Book of Quotations on Social Responsibility
- The Little Book of Quotations on Sustainable Business

The Little Book of Quotations on Transformational Change

Purpose Inspired: Reflections on Conscious Living: Volumes 1-5

Thriving: The Breakthrough Movement to Regenerate Nature, Society and the Economy

Fiction Books by Wayne Visser

I Am An African: Favourite Africa Poems

Wishing Leaves: Favourite Nature Poems

Seize the Day: Favourite Inspirational Poems

String, Donuts, Bubbles and Me: Favourite Philosophical Poems

African Dream: Inspiring Words & Images from the Luminous Continent

Icarus: Favourite Love Poems

Life in Transit: Favourite Travel & Tribute Poems

The Poetry of Business: A CEO's Quest for Meaning

Follow Me! (I'm Lost): The Tale of an Unexpected Leader

About the Author

Dr Wayne Visser is Professor of Integrated Value and holds the Chair in Sustainable Transformation at Antwerp Management School. He is Director of the think-tank and media company, Kaleidoscope Futures and Fellow at Cambridge University's Institute for Sustainability Leadership. His work as a strategy analyst, sustainability advisor, CSR expert, futurist and professional speaker has taken him to 77 countries. Dr Visser is author of 42 books – including *Thriving: The Breakthrough Movement to Regenerate Nature, Society and the Economy*. Dr Visser has been recognised as a top 100 thought-leader in trustworthy business and received the Global CSR Excellence & Leadership Award. He founded CSR International, after obtaining a PhD in corporate social responsibility. He previously served as Director of Sustainability Services for KPMG and Strategy Analyst for Capgemini in South Africa. Dr Visser lives in Cambridge, UK.

Website: www.waynevisser.com

Email: wayne@waynevisser.com

#Climatech.

Cleantech has been big and growing for a decade. Now there is a sub-category that is taking off: climatech. There were over 350 funding deals for climate-tech startups in 2020, with climate tech investments growing at five times the venture capital market over the past seven years. Examples include $600 million in early-stage funding for Swedish battery company Northvolt, $110 million for carbon-capture startup Climeworks, and $140 million for indoor farming entrepreneurs Plenty. And there is more to come, with Amazon pledging $2 billion and Microsoft $1 billion for climate tech.

#Timbuctoo.

Can you spot the next Timbuctoo? The town was established in 1885 at the height of the California gold-rush and was said to be named after an African American miner who came from Timbuktu in Mali. But as soon as gold fever subsided, the briefly thriving community became a ghost town. I wonder whether, metaphorically, the coal and oil industry will be the next Timbuctoo? Or will the internal combustion engine die out first? Will we look back on the fossil fuel era as a 200-year boom-and-bust aberration, just like those abandoned mining towns? Are there any other contenders?

#Marshmallows.

Do you have a marshmallow brain? I'm not being rude; it turns out we all do. In 1972, Stanford University conducted an experiment with children, offering them a marshmallow or similar treat. If they waited for 15 minutes before eating it, they would get another one. Two thirds could not resist the temptation. Roman Krznaric, in his book *The Good Ancestor*, calls this short-term reward orientation our marshmallow brain. But he says we also have an acorn brain – the ability to think long term, plan for the future and defer gratification. We're caught in a battle: marshmallow vs acorn.

#Prize.

If ever there was a techno-optimist, it's Elon Musk. And unlike others, his belief in the power of innovation has a track record of success, with PayPal, SpaceX and Tesla. Now Musk is funding a $100 million XPRIZE for whoever, in the next four years, comes up with a scalable technology that can remove carbon from the Earth's biosphere. This may be just the boost that carbon capture and storage (CCS) advocates need, after years of multinational and government investment and very little to show for it. If nothing else, it will inject urgency and creativity into climate solutions.

#Essence.

The best ideas are ones that capture the essence of something; a fundamental truth, or characteristic or aspiration. As Einstein put it, "everything should be made as simple as possible, but no simpler." One master of the art is architect Bill McDonough who recently turned 70. Many concepts that he has coined or co-developed capture the essence of important ideas. For example, technical and biological nutrients in circular flows, buildings as living organisms and the three types of carbon – fugitive, durable and living. My favourite is: let's strive to love all the children of all species for all time.

#Discounting.

Did you know that your children are regularly given the value of slaves; your grandchildren even worse? Under the US Constitution of 1787, an African-American slave was assigned three-fifths of the value of a free white person when calculating congressional representation. Today, governments and business typically apply a 3% discount rate to investments. Hence an investment that would benefit 100 people today is thought to only benefit 60 people after 17 years, 23 people after 50 years and 5 people after 100 years, even if that investment has long term benefits, such as planting a forest or scaling renewables.

#Lobbying.

The meat and dairy lobby are increasingly out of step with the times. Their crusade against plant-based alternatives is not new. In the 1980s, German milk producers (the largest in Europe) felt threatened enough to apply legal pressure for the government to shut down small tofu entrepreneurs, like TofuTown (happily, today a 60-million-euro company). More recently, the dairy industry has prevented the producers of plant-based alternatives from using terms like ""oat milk" and "soya yoghurt"; and now with Amendment 171 they want to go even further. These are desperation tactics, like King Canute trying to hold back the tide.

#Blades.

Wind power is the second most impactful climate solution, according to Project Drawdown, but that doesn't mean that it is fully sustainable. LM Wind Power, a subsidiary of GE Renewable Energy, produces 14,000 blades every year for turbines that can supply energy to more than 11 million households. Some are massive — GE's Haliade-X blades are 107 meters long and weighs 50 tons each. The problem is they are made of fiberglass, polymers and core material that are not recyclable. Now DecomBlades, a consortium of Danish companies, is looking to change that and make wind turbines that are 100% circular.

#Criticism.

If you want to know how future-fit a company or industry is, take a look at how it responds to criticism. In Spain, Heura, one of Europe's fastest growing vegan companies, is being taken to court by the meat industry after it put up a billboard saying "A meat burger pollutes more than your car". By contrast, Hanegal A/S, a major meat producer in Denmark, has committed to make 85% of its portfolio plant-based by 2030, while Archer Daniels Midland Co partners with Brazil's Marfrig Global Foods SA, the world's largest hamburger producer, to produce and distribute plant-based burgers.

#Butts.

I must confess, litter drives me crazy — and the worst is cigarette butts. Not only are they unsightly and take up to 10 years to biodegrade, but 4.5 trillion cigarette filters enter the ocean each year, endangering wildlife that ingest the plastic (cellulose acetate) and heavy metals. There are three solutions. First, educate smokers and issue heavy fines for who litter. Second, redesign the cigarette filter, which greenbutts has already done, creating a natural, rapidly degrading butt. And third, use drones and algorithms to identify and pick up discarded filters, which has been tested by Kinetica with 98% accuracy.

#Kangina.

Food preservation is essential to extend access to nutritious produce, as well as to prevent food waste. But today most food packaging is plastic made from fossil fuels that end up in landfills, rivers and oceans and doesn't break down. As we begin to develop more sustainable alternatives, let's draw inspiration from the centuries-old practice from northern Afghanistan. They created sealable containers made from mud and straw called kangina which kept produce fresh for months. Today the answers will likely come from substituting plastic with bio-based and biodegradable packaging made from plants, mushrooms or even food waste.

#Embodied.

Embodied impact is a powerful concept. Products have embodied carbon, water and land use footprints, which are invisible to most customers. For example, a Beyond Meat Burger compared to a beef burger has a carbon footprint that is 13 times lower, a water footprint 59 times lower and a land use footprint 43 times lower. Lower is better, but is it enough? Can we have products with positive impacts, so the more we consume, the better the world becomes? I call these regenerative products. They are rare but increasingly possible. For example, Interface has two carbon negative carpet products.

#Blankets.

Did you have a favourite baby blanket? Blankets have always been a symbol of comfort, safety and security. But sometimes they are more than that. The AIDS Memorial Quilt weighs 54 tons and spans 1.2 million square feet. The Witness Blanket in the Canadian Museum for Human Rights in Winnipeg is smaller, at 40 feet, but no less powerful. It has the legal status of a living entity and displays hundreds of items representing more than 150,000 indigenous children that were removed from their families to Indian Residential Schools for assimilation into white society. Blankets can be living memories.

#Gequality.

Gender inequality, in this day and age, is crazy. And yet, as the 2021 WEF Gender Gap report shows, it persists. We are only 68% of the way to overall gender parity. It's worst in political empowerment (22%) and economic participation and opportunity (58%). It will take 267 years to close the gender-pay gap if current trends continue. In the fastest growing jobs, women are especially underrepresented: only 14% in cloud computing for example. COVID-19 has exacerbated this inequality, with more women losing their jobs (5%) than men (3.9%). Men, it's time to take up the cause of gequality.

#Breadfruit.

In the search for sustainable foods, breadfruit could be the next big thing. There are three main benefits. First, each tropical tree produces as much as 800 pounds of fruit per year, which means it can supply small farmers with good income. Second, each tree absorbs 1.5 tons of CO_2 as it grows. Third, because the trees are grown in agroforests – farms that have a diverse mix of trees – they help build healthy soil. That's why Patagonia Provisions is working with a a female-owned farm cooperative in Costa Rica to turn the perishable breadfruit into flour to make crackers.

#Offshore.

Could America leapfrog the rest of the world on offshore wind? That's Biden's plan. Currently the US only produces 42 MW from offshore wind, putting it in 9th place; the UK leads with 10,206 MW, narrowly ahead of China. Biden's goal is to increase capacity to 30,000 MW by 2030, enough to power 10 million homes with clean energy, while creating 44,000 jobs and avoiding 78 million metric tons of CO2, equivalent to taking 17 million cars off the road. Of course, the rest of the world will power ahead. This is a race to the top. Everyone wins.

#Reasons.

Plant-based is booming. The $13.6 billion market is expected to more than double to $35 billion by 2027. AT Kearney predicts that by 2040, 60% of meat will either be cultured (grown from cells) or plant-based. In some countries, like the UK, it is already mainstream, with a third choosing meat-reduced diets, from vegans and vegetarians (13%) or flexitarian (21%). The question is, why? UK research suggests ethics is the strongest driver (34.7%, including climate, environmental and animal welfare concerns), followed by health (31.7%) and religion (19.9%). In systems thinking we call this convergence: multiple reasons; a confluence of trends.

#Travel.

What if you could visit a place that you have contributed to rewilding? That's the powerful idea behind the Nature & Carbon Corridors Project, which is a partnership between Exodus Travels and Rewilding Europe. The project aims to rewild 5,000 hectares of the Italian Apennines over the course of five years by creating nature corridors that link up surrounding national parks. On average 100 square metres of land will be rewilded for every passenger on every Exodus trip. Rather than buying carbon offsets, for the conscious traveller, it's a chance to make a positive impact and witness the change.

#ROC.

Most agriculture today is somewhere between a ROC and a hard place. ROC in this case stands for Regenerative Organic Certified. It is the latest and most ambitious third-party certification scheme, developed by Patagonia, the Rodale Institute and Dr. Bronner's. While we already have organic (or bio), fairtrade, Rainforest Alliance and other eco-labels, ROC focuses on the highest standards for soil health, animal welfare and farmworker fairness. Regenerative agriculture, including crop rotation, no-till cultivation and organic fertiliser, is still at the early stages, and developing standards is an important step towards maturity.

#Infrastructure.

Economies are built on good infrastructure but making these investments is always a bold and risky political move. Infrastructure is seldom cheap – Biden's American Jobs Plan has a $2.25 trillion price tag – and while it creates jobs in the short term, the biggest share of benefits is not immediate. Biden's plan includes a $174 billion investment in the EV market and aims to have 40 percent of the benefits of climate and clean infrastructure investments accrue to disadvantaged communities. This is the mark of true leadership: making decisions today that will benefit the future, even after you are gone.

#Rainwater.

Sometimes the solutions are so simple and effective that governments should just mandate them. Rooftop solar is one example; rainwater tanks are another. In Bermuda, where water is seen as a precious resource, regulations specify that 80 percent of each roof must be designated to catch the rain, and for every 10 square feet of roof, the tank below must hold 100 gallons of water. The roofs have a terraced design and are made with locally abundant limestone. This slows the water flow, keeps the house cool and makes the roofs practically hurricane proof. It's simple, smart and water-wise.

#Repairable.

Built-in-obsolescence is a big problem. Products are deliberately designed to have a limited life and to be unrepairable when they start to fail. That's been good for manufacturers, who get to sell more stuff, but it's catastrophic for the environment and expensive for customers. For example, of the 50 million metric tons of electronic waste generated annually, less than 20% is recycled and $57 billion in precious metals and raw materials are lost. The right-to-repair legislation in Europe and the UK is a great step forward and now needs to go global. Make it, break it, take it, repair it.

#Fanplastic.

For decades, the chemicals industry has been telling us how fantastic plastic is. In recent years, this has included PR about how plastic can save energy and be recycled. There is truth to both arguments. But this still fails to resolve the bigger problems of ocean plastic, microplastics, leaching of endocrine-disrupting chemicals and propping up the fossil fuel industry. They want their sustainability claims to be taken seriously, yet they are already lobbying against the newly proposed Break Free from Plastic Pollution Act in the US. They can't have it both ways. Either make plastic safe and sustainable or get rid of it.

#Navigation.

Faster isn't always better. At least not for the planet; often not for people either. Think of the slow food and slow fashion movements. Now Google may be seeding the slow drive movement when its Maps navigator will default to the greenest route, meaning the one with the lowest carbon emissions. If the time difference is significant, it will give you the option to choose faster or greener. This is a version of the Victory Speed Limit that slowed down cars during World War II to save on fuel. I hope the e-commerce and delivery companies follow Google's lead.

#Snownyms.

How many words are there for 'snow' in different languages? The Inuit people of Alaska have 70, while the Saami of northern Scandinavia and Russia have 180. Surprisingly, Scotland takes the prize with 421 words for snow, including 'feefle' (swirling snow), 'flindrikin' (a brief snow shower) and 'spitters' (small flakes of wind-driven snow). I celebrate these words as a tribute to nature's incredible diversity, with all its shapes and moods, its colours and rhythms. Personally, I'm drawn to warmer parts of the globe, especially the tropics. I'm enticed knowing that the Hawaiians, for example, have 20 words for 'rainbow'.

#Bridges.

At its best sustainability is like a bridge between the present and the future. It takes care of the present without compromising the needs of future generations. But not all bridges are alike. The Arkadiko stone bridge in Greece is believed to be over 3,000 years old. The principles of sustainable development – like social justice and environmental integrity – need to be like this: solid and unchanging. But the 500-year-old Root Bridges of Cherrapunji in India are grown. Sustainable solutions – including technology innovations, social behaviours, government policies and civil movements – need to be like this: constantly adapting and organically renewing.

#Femexec.

Research has shown that companies with more women in senior positions are more profitable, more socially responsible, and provide safer, higher-quality customer experiences. New research published in Harvard Business Review gives some clues as to why. First, women encourage more openness to change and simultaneously less risk taking. Second, women shift the focus from knowledge-buying to knowledge-building. It seems women may be better at developing strategies and building capacities for long-term value creation, rather than the get-rich-quick thinking that still dominates the male boardrooms of today. Diversity is smart – and right.

#Tax.

One of the most powerful government levers for change are taxes. But changing taxes is almost always unpopular. Even so, that doesn't look like it's going to stop President Joe Biden from trying. Besides increasing corporation tax and eliminating all subsidies, loopholes, and special foreign tax credits available to the fossil fuel industry, he is increasing the minimum tax payable for offshore profits. Biden is also mounting a campaign to persuade all governments around the world to impose a minimum corporate tax, to tackle the pervasive tax avoidance of multinationals that locate head-offices or operations in tax haven countries.

#Fishy.

As the Netflix documentary Seaspiracy continues to make waves, I am conflicted. Showing the devastating impacts of industrialized fishing is absolutely necessary and valuable. This should be the main takeaway from the film. The implication that sustainability labels like the Marine Stewardship Council are part of some secret conspiracy to support unsustainable fishing is, to put it politely, a red herring. Most disappointing of all is the lack of solutions. Telling 3 billion people to stop eating fish is naïve (and I speak as a vegan). The fishing industry is unsustainable and needs transforming. Let's stay focused on how.

#Inclusive.

How do we make carbon markets more inclusive? One way is to support the newly launched Inclusive Carbon Standard, which was developed by Food & Trees for Africa and Promethium Carbon. The open-source standard wants to help local communities access global carbon markets, notably by cutting the costs of carbon project development by at least a factor of 10, while still using approved methodologies. They foresee the inclusion of smart contracts using blockchain and measuring of carbon projects with multiple, everyday devices using the internet of things. Details on the standard are still lacking, but I want it to succeed.

#E-health.

The COVID pandemic has shown that we can do more online than we ever thought possible. It's no surprise that e-retailers like Amazon have thrived – and now they look set to disrupt another industry: healthcare. What if your Amazon Prime subscription came with a free same-day doctor's appointment? Since its announcement in March, Amazon's vision has become clearer. It plans to offer 24/7 chat access to clinicians, telemedicine access, in-home diagnostics, health provider house calls in select cities, and prescription drug delivery. All, most likely, at the easy click of a button. Incumbent healthcare providers must adapt or die.

#Halving.

In 2018, the world's top climate scientists at the IPCC told us that we will need to cut carbon emissions by 50% by 2030 to stay on track for meeting the Paris Climate Agreement target of net zero by 2050. The EU and UK were the first to take up the challenge. Then big business added their voice to the call, with more than 300 American companies – from Apple and Coca-Cola to Nike and Walmart – asking Biden to listen to the science and commit to 50% cuts by 2030. Biden listened and now other companies and countries must follow.

#Peak.

If we want a sustainable future, there are many things that need to peak and then decline. Coal consumption already peaked in 2013, and we need peak oil and peak gas to follow sooner rather than later. A new one is peak meat, which is expected by 2025 in Europe and North America, according to a report by Boston Consulting Group and Blue Horizon called 'Food for Thought'. Globally, by 2035 one in ten people will be eating 'alt protein', thereby saving the equivalent of Japan's annual carbon emissions and London's water supply for 40 years. That's peak performance.

#Wages.

In 1914, Henry Ford more than doubled the wages of his employees, effectively distributing $10 million in profits to his workers. His philosophy was that paying employees better made them more likely to afford the cars they were making. It was a virtuous cycle, a race to the top. Yet for the past 50 years, most multinationals have been chasing the lowest cost labour. A coalition of 10 global companies – led by IDH: The Sustainable Trade Initiative and including Fairphone, L'Oréal and Unilever – want to revive Ford's practice by committing to pay a living wage throughout their supply chains.

#Dice.

We are gambling on our climate future – and all of life depends on the outcome. But we don't need to take that chance. Instead, we can stack the odds in our favour, starting with education on climate. I was recently introduced to the Climate Dice and like all the best ideas and inventions, it is simple and powerful. Climate change is no game, but the dice is a creative, fun way to encourage children and adults – in our schools, universities and workplaces – to talk about climate problems and solutions as a first step towards taking action. Let's get rolling.

#Takeoff.

For a number of years, EVs have been poised to take off. What few realise is that it's happening already. In Germany, Europe's largest auto market and the 4th largest in the world, in December 2019 plugin electric vehicles held a 4.0% share. By December 2020, despite the pandemic, EVs reached an incredible 26.6% share. Volkswagen led with their brands e-Golf, ID.3, e-Up! and ID.4, selling 46,200 vehicles, followed by Renault's ZOE (31,450) and Tesla (16,700). This is what happens with convergence; the system flips to a new state much quicker than people anticipate. The EV race is on.

#PDK.

Most plastic ends up in landfills, rivers and oceans. Circular plastics are the answer, if we can develop systems to collect and recycle them. But most plastics need virgin plastic added during the recycling process, to maintain quality and functionality. That could be about to change. The Lawrence Berkeley National Laboratory is working on Polydiketoenamine, or PDK. Unlike most plastics, PDK is not melted down by heat during recycling but by acid, in such a way that the polymers and the additives can be separated. The result is plastic that can be 100% recycled an infinite number of times.

#Thrive.

Sooner or later, all companies have to go beyond sustainability to regeneration. Thrive Market plans to be the first online retailer to get that right. They have been carbon neutral since starting in 2010 and are already a strong supporter of regenerative agriculture and fair trade. Now they have set three ambitious goals for 2025: 1) to be climate positive (including their supply chain), 2) to be zero waste certified, and 3) to be plastic neutral (reducing plastic as much as possible and supporting collection projects like Plastic Bank to offset the balance). Is this the future of retail?

#Glass.

As a packaging material, glass has some downsides – it's heavy, so it takes more energy to transport, and it breaks. On the upside, it's made from natural materials (sand, soda ash and limestone) and can be reused and recycled back into glass. A lesser known option is that glass can be used to help mitigate coastal erosion. This is what Glass Half Full in Louisiana is planning to do. Their grassroots recycling program is collecting glass bottles from New Orleans' many restaurants and bars and turning them back into sand to restore lost coastline. From bottles to ecosystem restoration.

#Cicadas.

Nature is full of ingenious tricks in the struggle for life and the perennial battle between predator and prey. This year, billions of Brood X cicadas will emerge and swarm across the eastern United States, something that last happened 17 years ago. The cicada species has evolved this unusual decade-spanning life cycle so that its natural predators cannot anticipate its arrival en-mass, thus increasing the chances of successful breeding before they burrow underground for another 17-year hibernation. This is what Darwin meant by survival of the fittest; it's not the strongest that survive, it's those that adapt most creatively.

#Wealth.

The gap between rich and poor is large and growing in almost every country. In America, the richest 1% gained $7 trillion in wealth in 2020. The most effective way to address the problem is taxing the rich. But what kind of tax, and how much? There is an emerging support for a one-off wealth tax – including on property and financial stocks. In America, such a wealth tax – such as a 5% tax on the richest 5% of households (with wealth in excess of $2.5 million) is favoured across the political spectrum, according to recent polls.

#Metaverse.

You've probably heard of the multiverse – the scientific theory of multiple, parallel universes. Semiconductor company Nvidia and others like Roblox are taking that idea and looking at how to turn it into reality – or, to be more precise, into virtual reality. Nvidia's vision of what they call a metaverse is a digital twin – an identical computer-based replica - for everything in our world. This means that the buildings and factories of every city will have a digital twin that will simulate and track the physical version of it. Initially, this will be for gaming, but other possibilities are endless.

#Genomics.

The rapid development of COVID vaccines was made possible by genomics, the science of genetic sequencing. The leading tech company behind the gene decoding equipment is Illumina, which produced its first commercial genome in 2006 at a cost of $150,000. Today, it can sequence a human genome in an hour for $600 and they expect to get that down to $100 in the near future. This is not only good news for treating infectious diseases. Cancer researchers and others are benefiting as well. The more accessible genomics becomes, the better chance we have of achieving inclusive healthcare for all.

#Inflection.

If you are interested in system change, it helps to pay attention to inflection points. These are symbolic moments when key thresholds are reached. For example, on Christmas Day in 2009, Amazon customers bought more e-books than printed books. More recently, we have seen significant sustainability inflection points. In July 2020, Tesla became the world's most valuable carmaker, despite accounting for less than 1% of all cars sold. And in October 2020, the market capitalisation of NextEra, the world's largest generator of wind and solar power, eclipsed the oil giant ExxonMobil. For the times they are a'changin' (thanks Bob!).

#Rocketwoman.

The Elton John biopic Rocketman takes its title from his 1972 song. I'm a fan of the song and the artist, but I'm guessing when you hear 'rocket man', you might think of someone else, like Elon Musk, founder of SpaceX. My question is: where are all the rocket women? 65 women have flown in space since Russian cosmonaut Valentina Tereshkova broke the glass sky in 1963. Do we even know their names? How about Gwynn Shotwell – have you heard of her? She's not an astronaut, but she is president and COO of SpaceX. Let's start celebrating these sheroes.

#Oats.

Do you know what sold more than hand sanitiser in the first weeks of the pandemic? Cartons of Oatly – the original oat-derived milk substitute Swedish brand. That's because they have a shelf life of up to one year. No doubt they were also riding the plant-based wave, and now they have achieved a $1.4 billion IPO. Others are scrambling to catch up, like Danone with its established Alpro brand, Nestlé with its new pea-based alt-milk called Wunda, and US yoghurt manufacturing giant Chobani with its aspirations to lead on oat-based drinks. As an oat-drink-loving vegan, I'm cheering the competition.

#Tracking.

The boom in fitness tracking wearables and apps, like those from Fitbit, Garmin and Apple, are providing invaluable personal data to help individuals improve their health. Besides the direct health benefits, more and more providers of health and life insurance are offering discounts for those who share their tracked data on physical activity. Studies show that 150 minutes of activity per week can add 3.4 years to a person's life expectancy and reduce the risk for 13 different types of cancer. Now fitness tracking app Strava is sharing anonymised data with city planners to improve jogging and cycling paths.

#Forward.

When I came across the term 'fashion-forward' recently, I didn't know what it meant. It sounds a bit like 'pay-it-forward' and was linked to the footwear brand Rothy's conversion of 100 million water bottles into colourful shoes, so I did some checking. According to the Cambridge dictionary, it refers to things that will soon become very popular or fashionable. That's different to what I thought, but I like the meaning just as much. To consolidate its fashion-forward moniker, Rothy's has set an ambitious recycling goal to achieve fully circular production by 2023. Which other brands qualify as forward-fashion pioneers?

#Gazumping.

I'd like to repurpose this weird and wonderful word. It refers to offering a higher price on a property, after the seller already verbally agreed to a lower offer by someone else. So it's a form of out-bidding. I think lots of companies (even cities and countries) are going to be gazumped on sustainability. For example, sports retailer ASICS pledged to eliminate virgin polyester by 2030, to tackle the plastic pollution crisis. But Adidas gazumped them by committing to reach the same goal by 2024 and already offering two athletic fabrics created with 100% recycled polyester (Primeblue and Primegreen).

#IP.

I don't believe in an IP-free world, but exceptional circumstances call for exceptional responses. There is a strong case – both moral and pragmatic – to ease intellectual property restrictions on COVID vaccines. Pharmaceutical companies still need to recover R&D investments, but governments also invested heavily in Coronavirus vaccine development, as well as the rDNA science on which many vaccines are based. Loosening IP protections, which the US government now supports, would allow global manufacturing to scale more rapidly, thus increasing access to the vaccine for more than 7 billion people who still need it. Millions of lives are at stake.

#Sentience.

The more we learn about nature's wonders, the more we are rediscovering sentience. Since time immemorial, people accepted the sentience of all life – that trees and animals have souls, rivers and mountains have spirits, and the Earth itself is alive. More recently, materialistic science dismissed these beliefs as superstition and ignorance. But new science is revealing that animals have emotions, fish feel pain and trees have intelligence. In New Zealand, the Whanganui River has been granted legal personhood and in Ecuador, the people of Sarayaku are appealing to the highest court to recognise the sentience of their rainforest.

#Algorithms.

Automating decisions, by definition, takes humans out of the equation. With that comes the risk that ethics are removed as well. Artificial intelligence (AI) is prone to dehumanising effects: automated trading chasing the highest returns ignores social impacts, such as devastating the livelihoods of small farmers; racial biases in facial recognition software can lead to false convictions; CV screening by computers may result in discriminatory hiring; and predictive policing is vulnerable to racist profiling. And then we see Google firing the co-lead of their AI ethics team, Timnit Gebru, for being critical. Big Tech needs to start taking accountability.

#Wood.

Every year we cut down 15 billion trees, most from unsustainably managed forests. At the same time, restoring and protected forests is a natural climate solution that we are desperate to scale. It would help immensely if we could decrease the demand for trees – and now we can. Not by decreasing the use of wood, but by 3D printing wood products from waste sawdust and lignin, which the timber industry currently sends to landfill by the hundreds of millions of tons. Forust is gearing up to do this: 3D printing beautifully grained wood products from waste with zero waste.

#Looop.

Imagine if you could drop off your old clothes at a favourite retail shop and collect new ones the next day, which have been made from the recycled garments. This is what H&M is already doing at a store in Stockholm, using a machine called Looop, which automatically sterilises and shreds any old fabric, turning it into yarn and knitting it into a new piece of clothing chosen by the customer. The process uses no water or chemicals and is finished within eight hours. Looop may be a gimmick for now, but it's educating customers about the circular economy.

#Landscrapers.

For a century now, in the wake of Chicago and Manhattan's rise, cities have been worshipping the skyscraper. It became a symbol of modernity and wealth, with many countries competing to construct the tallest shopping malls, the highest apartment towers and the shiniest office blocks. But skyscrapers are not human scale. Like cathedrals before them, high-rise buildings are designed to impress and intimidate, rather than to be to nurture and welcome. Perhaps it is time to embrace what British urban designer Thomas Heatherwick calls landscrapers, like the low-rise Google UK campus he is building with a 300-metre rooftop park.

#Oaks.

Have you ever planned 150 years ahead? In Sweden they have. In the middle of Vättern, Sweden's second largest lake, is an oak-forested island called Visingsö. In 1870, the Swedish Crown planted 300,000 trees on the island, which it expected to harvest 150 years later for its ship building industry. Of course, by that time, wooden ships had all but disappeared. We can't stop the world from changing. Still, I admire their long-term thinking. The forest can still be harvested for timber, although I hope it will be saved as a regenerated ecosystem for eco-tourism, carbon sequestration and wildlife.

#Coolants.

The quickest way to cool the climate is to get rid of coolants. That may sound like a paradox, but it's true. When the hydrofluorocarbon (HFC) gases we use in refrigeration and air conditioners leak, they have a global warming effect thousands of times stronger than CO_2. Now the US Environmental Protection Agency plans to cut their production and use by 85% in 15 years, which is broadly in line with the global Kigali Amendment. And since HFCs do not last a long time in the atmosphere (unlike CO_2), the benefits of cutting them would be seen more quickly.

#Mangroves.

It's becoming clear that blue carbon – CO_2 stored in lakes and oceans – is more promising for carbon sequestration than land-based natural climate solutions like tropical forests. One particularly productive source of blue carbon is the protection and restoration of coastal mangrove forests. Conservation International is working with Apple to preserve a 27,000-acre mangrove forest in Colombia and P&G to safeguard 110,000 acres of forest in the Philippines. Besides storing a lot of carbon (4-10 times more than terrestrial forests), mangroves have the advantage that they are less likely to be destroyed through forest fires or logged for timber.

#Jewellery.

In Greek mythology, when Pandora opened her box it unleashed misery and evil in the world. The same might be argued for our modern-day jewellery boxes. Mining for diamonds and other jewels is often associated with dangerous working conditions, massive environmental impacts and financing conflict. The strangest thing is that all this negative impact is entirely unnecessary. Lab-grown diamonds are identical to those dug up from the earth and much more sustainable. Finally, the industry – and the customers it serves – seems to be waking up to this, with Danish jewellery manufacturer Pandora launching its first lab-grown, carbon neutral collection.

#Bonding.

At last, finance for sustainability is starting to stick. One indicator of this is the boom in green, climate and social bonds, which are expected to exceed $1 trillion in 2021. This simple financial instrument – effectively, a loan taken by a company from multiple investors with a fixed date of repayment – is proving to be a powerful agent of change. Amazon recently issued a $1 billion bond to finance initiatives across five focus areas: renewable energy, clean transport, sustainable buildings, affordable housing and socio-economic empowerment. Sustainability bonds combine a safe financial return with a positive social return on investment.

#Plans.

Increasingly, stakeholders – including shareholders – want to know what a company's long term plan on sustainability is; and more especially on climate change. It used to be that business avoided publishing ambitious goals, fearing a backlash from financial markets. Now, the opposite is true. Unilever's Climate Transition Action Plan – which was approved by 99% of shareholders on 5 May – includes a $1 billion climate and nature fund, net zero carbon by 2039 and halving the footprint of their products by 2030. Laggards, like Barclays' shareholders rejecting rapid divestment from fossil fuels, will only increase their transition risk and decrease their competitiveness.

#Particulates.

Every year, fossil fuel related air pollution kills more than 8 million people (18% of global deaths). The main cause is PM2.5 – particulate matter that is two-and-a-half microns or less in width – which aggravates respiratory conditions like asthma and can lead to lung cancer, coronary heart disease and strokes. In addition, COVID deaths are higher in areas with worse levels of PM 2.5. Less well known is that agriculture is also a major source of air pollution, accounting for 15,900 premature deaths annually, 80% of which are linked to ammonia emissions from livestock waste and fertilizer in meat production.

#Wool.

I must confess, I'm not a fan of any livestock farming. But I'm also a pragmatist, and in the search for climate positive, circular solutions, it seems like wool is making a strong case. Sheep Inc. has demonstrated that by using regenerative agriculture on their sheep farms in New Zealand, they sequester enough carbon to make their hoodies carbon negative, taking into account their full life cycle impacts. They go further by using renewable energy and avoiding chemical additives so that their products are fully biodegradable. The carbon dividends from regenerative farming could transform the fashion and textiles industry.

#Scarcity.

We all know that we live on a finite planet with scarce resources, but our obsession with efficiency has also created artificial scarcity – and less resilience. Take the recent shortage of computer chips affecting the electronics and automotive industries. We blame the pandemic, but really this is the result of a decades-long pursuit of just-in-time inventory management. Big brand companies outsource production and keep close to zero stock. That saves money, but it also means there are no products available when crises disrupt production. This a classic lesson in resilience, where systems always require slack capacity or built-in redundancy.

#Rocks.

Enhanced weathering of rocks could speed up carbon capture and help tackle climate change. When dissolved CO2 in rain falls on basalt rock, the chemical reaction creates a carbonate mineral that effectively sequesters carbon indefinitely. The problem is that, in nature, this is a very slow and location-dependent process. But The Future Forest Company is starting an experiment that will crush basalt rocks and spread them in a forest on the Scottish Isle of Mull. By increasing the area of exposed basalt, the weathering process is accelerated, while the remineralised soil could boost forest growth by up to 40%.

#Hybrid.

After the pandemic forced home-working for many, do we want to go back to the office? Yes, but less. Research by the Universities of Chicago and Essex found that remote workers worked 30% longer hours with no increase in productivity, and in the US, depression and anxiety quadrupled to 40% of all adults. On the other hand, a Harvard study found 81% of professions would prefer a hybrid work schedule, and companies that have tested a 4-day week have found productivity increases of between 20% (at New Zealand's Perpetual Guardian) and 40% (in a limited trial at Microsoft Japan).

#Mosquitos.

The experiment with GMO mosquitos being conducted in the Florida Keys is controversial, but are we being over-cautious? The project by UK biotech firm Oxitec aims to replicate its success in Brazil, where introducing a 'self-limiting' gene caused mosquito populations to fall by 95% in similar tests. Mosquito-borne diseases kill over a million people a year and climate change will increase habitats conducive to its spread. The concern is that there may be unintended consequences when we manipulate nature. But we are doing this already, using chemical pesticides that we know have harmful side-effects on human and ecological health.

#Queer.

Fast Company's 2021 Queer 50 got me thinking about what we are celebrating in Pride Month. This is the second annual ranking of top LGBTQ women and nonbinary innovators in business and tech. The Q50 list was created in collaboration with Lesbians Who Tech & Allies and features leaders like Alicia Garza, founder of Black Futures Lab, Sally Susman, Chief Corporate Affairs Officer at Pfizer, and Jen Wong, COO of Reddit. In my view, gender identity and sexual preference shouldn't matter – but it still does, because of discrimination. So, let's celebrate leaders who overcome prejudice to achieve great things.

#Compensation.

What are we going to do about CEO pay – or don't we really care? Most people agree with the principle of fair compensation. And most also agree that CEOs earning 320 times the average worker (in 2019) is not fair. Yet we don't seem to be doing anything about it. The gap increased in 2020, with CEO pay rose 16%, compared with 1.8% for workers in the largest 350 companies. Is this a failure of policymakers in the pocket of multinationals, or of civil action that couldn't sustain the Occupy movement? Tackling inequality has to start inside the company.

#Shells.

How can we take 10 billion tons of carbon out of circulation every year? It's a trillion dollar question and start-up company Seachange has an answer: make more seashells, more quickly. The formation of calcium carbonate shells is a natural process that locks away carbon for millions of years. Their technology, so far only lab-tested, draws seawater through a mesh, giving it an electric charge that triggers the necessary chemical reaction. Unlike the air, the ocean has much higher carbon concentrations and the sequestration process takes less energy. Seachange estimates that 1,800 of their shell-making devices could be enough.

#Polio.

We don't often get a lot of good news being reported on Africa. But here is some. In 1988, polio, a disease that causes paralysis mainly among children under 5 years of age, was endemic in 125 countries. In the 1990s, around 75,000 children were paralysed by polio every year. Last year, Nigeria was the last country in Africa to be declared polio free. This is the result of the Kick Polio Out of Africa campaign that was launched in 1996 by Rotary International, together with UNICEF, WHO and others. In 2020, only Afghanistan and Pakistan still have polio.

#Fractals.

Nature is full of patterns and the most pervasive – and many might say, the most beautiful –are fractals. These are patterns that repeat at different scales, illustrating mathematically precise relationships like the Fibonacci sequence. We see fractals everywhere, from the spirals of sunflowers, seashells, and fern fronds to the vortices of whirlpools, hurricanes, and galaxies. There are echoing patterns in the structure of leaves, the network of human veins and the branches of trees, river deltas and glacier meltwaters. I find it comforting that there is order in the apparent chaos of life, and in that order, beauty too.

#Herstory.

History is often just that – his story, a record of the exploits of (and exploitations by) men. Women are almost invisible in history, so perhaps it needs retelling, as herstory. For example, we know that Watson and Crick discovered DNA, but seldom hear about Rosalind Franklin whose data was critical to their breakthrough. When we think of the Black Panther Party, we probably bring to mind the fisted salute of defiant men. Now, a 30-foot tall mural on a house in West Oakland, California, is paying tribute to the women who fueled the movement. Let's stop history repeating itself.

#HyXchange.

Hydrogen will play a significant role in the energy transition to a net zero carbon economy. The Netherlands is planning a new financial exchange, called HyXchange, which will track the price of hydrogen and allow trading of hydrogen commodities. Crucially, the price index will show the hydrogen's source and the carbon-volume involved in its production, and hydrogen certification to choose between green hydrogen (produced by electrolysis of water using renewable energy sources), blue hydrogen (produced by steam methane reforming, together with technologies for CO_2 capture) or yellow hydrogen (using nuclear-generated electricity).

#Producers.

Who is responsible for the impact of our products? Increasingly, it looks like the buck will stop with producers. The concept of extended producer responsibility (EPR) is not a new one. For example, in electronics there have been EPR requirements in Europe since the 2012 WEEE Directive. Now the momentum is growing for the same approach to be applied to the packaging industry. More than 100 significant players in packaging value chain – from Danone, Diageo, L'Oreal and Nestle to Pepsi, Coca-Cola, Unilever and Walmart – have signed an Ellen MacArthur Foundation statement calling for greater EPR alignment, policies and actions.

#Renewables.

The throw-away economy has higher environmental impacts and costs more. It's obvious when you say it like that, but it seems that consumer products companies still need convincing. A new study called 'Reuse wins' by Upstream has crunched the numbers, comparing the life cycle impacts of disposables versus reusables in the food services sector and found that, on almost every environmental measure, reuse is better. For example, disposable cups have a 3-10 times higher carbon footprint and 7 times higher water footprint. That's before we factor in issues like waste and resource use. Reuse also save food businesses money.

#Seafood.

You're probably thinking fish, lobsters and prawns, right? But seafood is also going plant-based, with the rise of seaweed cuisine. In Asia, it's a popular ingredient in many dishes, but it is also starting to be used by alt-protein companies to make plant-based seafood. The beauty of seaweed is that it is a zero input food, requiring no external resources, it grows incredibly fast (around 20 centimetres a month) and it is a natural climate solution. A typical farm like gimMe's in South Korea produces around 3 tonnes of seaweed a month, sequestering up to 12 tonnes a year.

#Parking.

Joni Mitchell could be hailed as a prophet when she sang 'they paved paradise and put up a parking lot' in her 1970 song, Big Yellow Taxi. In America today, there are eight parking spaces for every car. California has a bill pending to stop building regulations from prescribing minimum amounts of parking. Think of all the space that could be freed up for nature and the community if that was reduced to a one-to-one ratio, let alone if we cut overall car use by making cycling, scootering, public transport, car sharing and taxis more convenient, affordable and pleasurable.

#Ecocide.

Soon, the international criminal court (ICC) may add ecocide to the four offenses that it already prosecutes (war crimes, crimes against humanity, genocide and the crime of aggression). Legal experts from across the globe, working under the banner of the Stop Ecocide Foundation, are proposing the ecocide be defined as "unlawful or wanton acts committed with knowledge that there is a substantial likelihood of severe and widespread or long-term damage to the environment being caused by those acts". If draft law is adopted by ICC's members, it will be a watershed historical moment, both for humanity and the planet.

#Photosynthesis.

Scientists have been trying to copy the photosynthesis capabilities of plants since at least 1883 when New York inventor Charles Fritts created the first solar cell. Since then, solar panel efficiency has risen from 1% to around 20% today, with protypes pushing that number to 45%. But what if we could go back to the source and increase the photosynthesis of plants themselves – and especially trees in forests – which are natural carbon sinks. That's what biotech company Living Carbon is focused on. This is the dawn of the age of GMTs (genetically modified trees). Is that good or bad?

#Listening.

I recently heard a powerful slogan: nothing about us without us. The saying has historical roots dating back to the 1500s in central Europe but could not be more relevant today. When I work with companies on stakeholder materiality assessment, I often use the triple-test of power, legitimacy and urgency, because it serves as a good reminder not to only listen to those with a strong influence, or a loud voice. We also need to include the powerless, invisible and voiceless stakeholders, like young people, future generations and nature itself (comprising millions of organisms), all impacted by our actions.

#Next.

Western multinationals have struggled for decades to serve customers at the base of the economic pyramid in emerging markets. The hard-won lesson, it seems, is to engage in partnerships with established national companies. Google, for example, is betting that its new partnership with Reliance Jio, India's leading telecoms company, to launch an ultra-affordable smartphone called JioPhone Next will give an additional 520 million users access to the internet. This forms part of Google's $10 billion India Digitization Fund. Of course, Google is motivated by acquiring market share and making money, but it's also an important step in digital inclusion.

#Crunch.

We are entering the decade of resource crunches. Ironically, it is the rapid take-up of sustainable and renewable products and services that is driving resource scarcity, in everything from green hydrogen and the metals in batteries to recycled plastics and sustainable cotton. There are already significant bottlenecks, and these are sure to increase in the short term. But if there's one thing that markets are good at, it is balancing supply and demand. As a result, investments to increase the necessary flow of resources inputs for sustainable solutions will skyrocket in the next 10 years, creating a virtuous cycle.

#Carbochemicals.

These days, petrochemical is a dirty word, and rightly so, since it is associated with a dirty, pollution- and climate-causing industry. But chemistry itself is not inherently dirty. And much of what we derive from petrochemicals can be extracted from sources other than fossil fuels. The San Francisco start-up Twelve, for example, is using renewable electricity to perform industrial photosynthesis, a process that extracts useful chemical elements from carbon dioxide and water, and then turns these into the raw materials used in thousands of products. They're already working with Mercedes-Benz and Procter & Gamble, so scaling is already happening.

#Intolerance.

Inclusion is an often-overlooked reason to offer more plant-based options in schools, workplaces, restaurants, and hotels. In many cases, vegan food makes it easier to cater to faith-based requirements like halaal, kosher, or vegetarian. But according to the US Department of Health and Human Services, there are genetic factors as well, since around 30 to 50 million American adults are lactose intolerant and – something I never knew – this is more prevalent in minority populations, affecting 95% of Asians, 60-80% of African Americans, 80-100% of American Indians and 50-80% of Hispanics, as compared to 2% for those with European origins.

#Enzymatic.

Have you heard of enzymatically recycled plastic? If not, you can expect to hear a lot about it in the coming years. Enzymes are one of nature's most effective recycling agents. Recently, after 10 years of research, bio-industrial company Carbios successfully demonstrated that its compost-derived enzymes can break down 97% of plastic in 16 hours – 10,000 times faster than other similar trials have shown to date. The process has been successfully demonstrated by a consortium that includes L'Oreal, Nestlé and PepsiCo, which have made the world's first food-grade PET clear plastic bottles from enzymatically recycled, coloured and complex plastic.

#Ride.

The meteoric rise of Uber and Lyft became posters for the gig economy. But as evidence accumulated of poor workers' rights and inadequate pay for drivers, both companies lost their lustre. Co-op Ride is trying to change that by running as a co-operative, where the drivers own and control the company. As a result, the company takes less commission (15% vs Uber's 25%) and drivers earn 8-10% more per ride, as well as getting an annual dividend based on their labour – those who drove more, get a higher proportion of the profits. There's a lot to like about co-operatives.

#Crossing.

Our roads are death-traps for animals. That's why I celebrate every time I see a wildlife crossing – either a tunnel under or a bridge over a road that allows creatures to safely move around their habitat. Some take this interspecies courtesy even further, like Snake Road in southern Illinois. The gravel road, which lies between two sheer cliffs and forms part of the Trail of Tears Forest, is closed twice a year to allow reptiles and amphibians to migrate from the cliff to the nearby swamp and back. Wherever a road cuts through a habitat, wildlife crossings are needed.

#Steel.

When it comes to decarbonising, there are easy wins and hard challenges. Decarbonising electricity is relatively easy. Decarbonising steel production is hard. This is not a trivial problem since steel contributes 11% to global carbon emissions. We have some solutions, like green hydrogen, but they are still expensive. That's why partnerships are key. Volvo is working with Nordic steel producer SSAB to begin manufacturing its cars with fossil-free steel by 2026. By ensuring sufficient demand for its green steel, SSAB can commit to the necessary green hydrogen investments and start to bring down the costs through economies of scale.

#Snuggle.

The Darwinian notion of evolutionary competition is being replaced by a new understanding: the 'snuggle for survival'. Darwin borrowed the 'survival of the fittest' and the 'struggle for survival' from Herbert Spencer. What he meant, of course, was survival of the most adaptable. But evolutionary biologists are finding that competition in nature is the exception and cooperation is the rule. In a letter to New Scientist in 2009, Thomas Frost proposed that 'a mutation finds a niche and snuggles into it'. Similarly, in her book on natural intelligence, Leen Gorissen emphasises the prevailing mutualism of win-win relationships in nature.

#Data.

Knowledge is power – and data is the bedrock. With high resolution satellite imaging, anyone anywhere can track land use changes in near-real time. The empty promises of politicians and the polished rhetoric of corporations are easily exposed. Geophotographic data doesn't lie. I witnessed the power of knowledge, data, and storytelling at the launch of the #MoseMerrMalin campaign (Don't Take the Mountain) on deforestation in Kosovo. Interactive maps produced by CorrelAid Netherlands and Sustainability Leadership Kosova website show how this nature-rich country is losing 1.5 football fields of forest every day. Data inspires action.

#Returning.

Business leaders who think employees will be happy to return to office-work-as-usual are in for a big surprise. There is already talk of The Great Resignation, as people reconsider their options. Pre-COVID research by Stanford University of 16,000 employees found that working from home increased productivity by 13% and cut attrition in half. Admittedly, many are feeling online fatigue, and home offices are not ideal for those with young families or inadequate space and equipment. At the same time, many of us have come to value and expect the flexibility and time- and carbon-saving benefits of a mobile office.

#Design.

Many sustainable solutions today are little more than retrofitting outdated, unsustainable products and services. It's far better – easier, cheaper and more effective – to design for sustainability from the outset. This realisation has led to an unusual partnership between Johnny Ives, famous for his Apple product designs, Prince Charles, a consistent voice for sustainability, and the Royal College of Art in London. Their new Terra Carta Design Lab will challenge students to "create small designs that can make a big impact for the world's transition to a sustainable future", with funding from Amazon, Octopus Energy and the Islamic Development Bank.

#Heraean.

Sometimes, it is worth celebrating how far we have come. Women were banned from the original Olympic games in Greece. Those caught attending (let alone participating) were said to be cast down from Mount Typaeum and into the river flowing below. Happily, women have never been content to bow to the discriminatory dictates of men. The women of Greece set up their own athletics games, called the Heraean Games, in honour of Hera, the Greek goddess of women, marriage, family and childbirth. Even in 2021, gender equality in sport has not been achieved, but the Olympics shows the way.

#Pulp.

With the plastics industry in the dock for its disastrous impacts on nature, communities and health, the pulp and paper sector may be set to boom. Of course, not all plastics can be substituted by wood and paper pulp derived packaging, but a lot can. One example is the new partnership between Procter & Gamble (P&G) and the Paper Bottle Company (Paboco), which will launch paper bottles on the European market in 2022. In the case of detergents, the bottles will still have a plastic (recycled PET) inner bag and top, but the switch will cut plastic by 30%.

#Recovery.

If you think governments aren't delivering on climate promises in their economic recovery spending, you are absolutely right. An analysis by the International Energy Agency of more than 800 policy decisions from over 50 countries shows that only 2% of the COVID-19 stimulus funding promised has been spent on clean energy. This only represents 35% of the level of funding recommended by the IEA in its recent roadmap to net-zero by 2050. This is the time to increase the pressure on our elected officials, to make them accountable for their actions – or lack of action. Climate investment can't wait.

#Universal.

It's useful to distinguish between universal problems and global problems. Universal problems, like pollution or social injustice, occur everywhere but can and must be tackled locally. Global problems like climate change and tax avoidance have local causes but global effects and can only be tackled by international collaboration. For universal issues, there is a strong incentive to implement solutions since those affected can apply pressure and benefit directly from the changes. For global problems, it's much harder. They require systems thinking, cross-border solidarity. They demand selfless action and concern for distant communities and future generations.

#Engagement.

The only way to attract and retain talent is to keep employees engaged. This is easier said than done. According to Gallup, only 20-34% of worker in the US and Canada feel engaged, and disengagement costs around 18% of their annual salary in terms of lost productivity. And replacing disengaged workers requires one-half to two times the employee's annual salary. To cure this malignant malady, I propose a four-part PILL: ensure there is an engaging Purpose; make the tasks of jobs Interesting; offer plenty of Learning opportunities; and nurture Loyalty by making employees feel part of a caring community.

#Weedbots.

When demand for toxic chemicals like Agent Orange were no longer needed by America to wage war, the industry pivoted and started using them as agricultural herbicides, pesticides and fungicides. For 80 years, we have been poisoning the soil and wildlife with these chemicals, but that may be about to change. Robots that still use herbicides but with precision targeting can reduce chemical use by 90%. Or even better, the autonomous vehicles of Carbon Robotics can destroy 100,000 weeds an hour without any chemicals, only using lasers. Robots can be expensive, but FarmWise lease theirs for $200 per acre.

#Milk.

With the milk wars raging today (which is really a losing battle by dairy milk producers to stop plant-based alternatives from competing), it is worth remembering that stealing food meant for baby cows and goats was not always common practice. In Ancient Rome and Greece, those who drank milk and ate butter were seen as barbarians; poor people, often peasant farmers, who relied on their livestock for subsistence. The spread of affordable refrigeration in the twentieth century allowed perishable dairy products to reach a mass market. But now the move towards plant-based diets is once again marginalising cows' milk.

#Rental.

The sustainability benefits of shifting to a rental market fashion was recently brought into question. Finnish researchers performed a life cycle assessment (LCA) of a pair of jeans under five ownership and end-of-life scenarios, concluding that the rental option had higher carbon emissions than simply throwing the jeans away. There are two major lessons I take from this. First, the climate impact of transportation and logistics is still significant and should be factored into any sustainable solutions. And second, LCAs are limited by their scope. In this case, other important sustainability impacts like water and biodiversity were not considered.

#Unextracted.

It's time we started holding extractive companies accountable for their unrealistic and irresponsible plans. The latest scientific estimates, published in the Nature journal, are that 60 percent of oil and fossil methane gas, and 90 percent of coal must remain unextracted to keep within a 1.5 degrees Celsius carbon budget. Any oil and gas or mining company – or any national government – that bases their projected reserves and future revenues on digging up and burning any more than this is perpetuating a carbon bubble about to burst, leaving billions of dollars in stranded assets. The Great Carbon Disruption is upon us.

#Library.

We all have our unique stories to tell, but is there anyone willing to listen? It seems that, yes, there is. In the Human Library Project, 'readers' have a chance to spend 30 minutes with a human book – volunteers who share their personal experiences on particular themes, with hundreds of book titles ranging from ADHD, Alcoholic and Autism to Solider (PTSD), Unemployed and Young Mother. The project's by-line is "unjudge someone", which gives some insight into the diversity and inclusion goal that motivated its Danish founders in 2000. Today, there are human libraries in 80 countries in six continents.

#Rust.

When you think about the race for the next battery technology breakthrough, I bet you're not thinking about rust. But Form Energy, founded by a former Tesla employee, is betting on its iron-air battery, which converts iron to rust, then rust back into iron, discharging and charging the battery in the process. What's remarkable is how long the batteries can store electricity (around 100 hours), and the costs they expect to achieve when mass production begins in 2025, around $6 per kilowatt-hour of storage, compared to $50 to $80 per kWh for nickel, cobalt, lithium or manganese based batteries.

#Darkness.

We are familiar with nature reserves for wildlife and marine reserves in the ocean, but have you ever heard of a dark sky reserve? These are increasingly rare areas that are protected from light pollution, making them ideal for star gazing and nocturnal creatures. More than 80 percent of the world's population lives under light-polluted skies. That is why, in 2012 New Zealand established the 1,600 square mile Aoraki Mackenzie International Dark Sky Reserve. If you can stay at its off-grid Lakestone Lodge on the edge of brilliantly blue Lake Pukaki, the nearest traffic light is 100 miles away.

#Printers.

Wind turbines are rapidly changing the economics of renewable energy production, with offshore wind capacity expected to triple by 2025 and increase 15-fold by 2040, according to the IEA. But we also need to make the production of the turbines more sustainable. One way is to 3D print the component parts close to where they will be used. A new partnership between GE, Fraunhofer Institutes and Voxeljet AG will develop the world's largest 3D printer – a sand binder jet printer called the Advance Casting Cell – for offshore wind applications, like GE's Haliade-X, standing 248 metres high with 107-metre blades.

#Coal.

The collapse of the coal industry is already happening, despite what you may hear about China and India's continued plans to back the climate-wrecking fossil fuel. A report by E3G, Global Energy Monitor and Ember has found that more than three-quarters of the world's planned plants have been scrapped since the Paris Climate Agreement was signed in 2015. In fact, there are 44 countries that no longer have any future coal power plans. If China, India, Vietnam, Indonesia, Turkey and Bangladesh can be persuaded to commit to no new coal, the pipeline for future coal plants will drop 90%.

#Forever.

Diamonds are forever, but what if toxic chemicals are too? One of the most serious and least talked about crises we face is the accumulation of persistent chemicals in the environment. These so-called "forever chemicals", like PFAS (per- and polyfluoroalkyl substances), are used in everything from paints and cosmetics to food packaging to solar panels. PFAS chemicals, by design, do not biodegrade. So, it's no surprise that they are bio-accumulating in the food chain and ending up in human breast milk and our blood. Sometimes lasting forever, which is what 'sustainable' means, is the last thing we really want.

#Lobbyists.

The unhealthy influence of big business on government is undermining democracy the world over. But government officials are public servants who work for us, the voters who put them in place. They should be accountable for how they spend their time, and especially who they spend it with. In the UK, an investigation by the environmental group DeSmog found that British ministers met with fossil fuel companies nine times more than with clean energy companies over the past two years or so. This flies in the face of the government's climate policy for cutting emissions by 68% by 2030.

#Children.

We say we care for our children, but our actions betray us. In a survey for Avaaz of 10,000 young people from 10 countries (Australia, Brazil, Finland, France, India, Nigeria, the Philippines, Portugal, the UK), around 60% are very or extremely worried about climate change and believe that governments are not protecting them, the planet, or future generations. They feel betrayed by the older generation and governments. Around 40% are hesitant to contemplate having children in the face of climate catastrophe. These are sobering findings, but I view them through a lens of hope. The youth will demand change.

#Grasslands.

Tropical rainforests get all the glory – and to be fair, they are fabulous – but spare a thought for humble grasslands. When we lose grassland ecosystems, we lose natural carbon sinks that provide habitats for hundreds of species, reduce soil erosion and prevent downstream flooding. For example, millions of acres of America's Great Plains are being converted each year to grow corn, wheat and soy (primarily for biofuels and animal feed). That's why environmental groups are calling for the creation of a Grasslands Conservation Act and why WWF is working on a $6 million project to improve grassland grazing practices.

#Burnout.

According to a June 2021 Gallup poll, 74% of employees experience burnout on the job at least sometimes. The impact on individuals' wellbeing and economic security is significant. So too is the cost to employers in productivity loss and talent recruitment and retention, not to mention the erosion of workplace morale and company reputation. So how can we avoid burnout? Gallup's director of workplace management finds three clues among "burnout free" employees: 1) they are more engaged at work; 2) they have high wellbeing through work-life integration; and 3) they work in a culture that celebrates each person's strengths.

#Bitcoin.

Cryptocurrencies are here to stay, but until they address their astronomical ecological footprint, they don't deserve our support. According to a U.S. Environmental Protection Agency researcher, bitcoin mining produces 15 times more carbon than mining an equivalent amount of gold (in dollar value terms). In fact, Bitcoin consumes more energy than the whole of the Netherlands, and as much as all the datacentres in the world combined. And now research from economists at the Dutch central bank and MIT has found that every Bitcoin transaction also generates the equivalent of two iPhones in electronic waste. Secure, yes. Sustainable, no.

#Overview.

The Overview Effect is the name for the profound shift in consciousness that happens when astronauts see the Earth from space. Coined in 1987 in a book by Frank White, the effect itself dates back to the Apollo space missions in the early 1970s and their breath-taking "blue marble" photographs they captured. The latest to experience the effect is Jeff Bezos. Following his low orbit space flight with Blue Origin in July 2021, he described the Earth as "finite; both beautiful and fragile" and confirmed $1 billion of his $10 billion Bezos Earth Fund will go towards conservations projects.

#COP.

For some, the opening of COP26 – the global climate negotiations in Glasgow – on 31 October, Halloween, seems scarily apt. We face a nightmarish future if we fail to increase climate ambition and action by politicians, executives, and citizens. COP will bring its fair share of victories and disappointments, but I'd like to offer a systems thinking perspective. The COP process has all the hallmarks of the scientific principles of thriving. It is increasing complexity (meaning connectivity), circularity, coherence, creativity, convergence, and continuity. This is systems change in action, a virtuous cycle of positive reinforcing actions, nearing a tipping point.

#Trillion.

Tesla has become the latest company – and arguably the first company with a core sustainability mission – to be valued at over $1 trillion (that's $1,000,000,000,000), following an order of 100,000 Model 3 EVs by Hertz, simultaneously making CEO Elon Musk the richest person in the world. Tesla is the youngest in the trillion-dollar club, founded in 2003, joining Saudi Aramco (the only fossil legacy company), Microsoft, Apple, Amazon, and Alphabet/Google. Such concentration of power is a worrying trend, but also has the potential to speed the transition to a thriving future, if we ensure they use their impact wisely.

#Words.

At COP26, we will be inundated by a tsunami of words, as more than 120 world leaders put forward their plans and promises on climate action. It will be all too easy to say that their words are all just "bla bla bla" - empty rhetoric. But words matter. They are not actions, yet they are enablers for action, signals to business and citizens that big changes are coming, sooner rather than later. Biological systems are self-regulating and self-renewing – a characteristic known as autopoiesis. In social systems, networks of communication have the same function. Words amplify the urgency to act.

#India.

Indian Prime Minister Modi says India will only reach net zero by 2070, twenty years later than the Paris Climate Agreement goal. I disagree. While India only emits around 1.9 tonnes of CO_2 per person, compared with 15.5 tonnes for the US, India is already the fourth largest polluter (behind the China, the US and the EU). Yet, I am convinced that India will reach net zero by 2050. Why? Because it is part of a global system that is rapidly and irreversibly transforming. India will be driven by mounting social pressure, climate impacts, technology advances and market forces.

#Breakthroughs.

We won't create a climate positive future without innovation, including sustainable technologies deployed with unprecedented scale and speed around the world. Knowing this, at COP26 more than 40 countries representing two thirds of the global economy – including the US, Japan, China and India – have committed to the Glasgow Breakthrough Agenda. These are 2030 global goals that aim to make clean technologies and sustainable solutions the most affordable, accessible and attractive option in key emitting sectors – power, road transport, steel, hydrogen and agriculture. Add new commitments to end deforestation and cut methane 30% by 2030 and thriving looks increasingly possible.

#Finance.

Money talks. So, what do you think $130 trillion of climate finance might be saying? This is the amount of private capital committed by 450 financial companies from 45 countries, under the umbrella of the Glasgow Financial Alliance for Net Zero (GFANZ). How big is this? It is more than the world's total assets under management in 2020. The message is loud and clear. Banks are ready to fund the green industrial revolution – and they will be asking their corporate clients for credible, science-based transition plans for halving their emissions by 2030 and reaching net zero by 2050. Capiche?

#Activists.

As the world braces itself for ongoing climate protests, we need to celebrate and support social and environmental activist movements. Women are often at the forefront: inspiring climate activists like Greta Thunberg, Vanessa Nakate, Dominika Lasota and Mitzi Tan, but also courageous women like Esther Ze Naw Bamvo and Ei Thinzar Maung who are leading anti-military protests in Myanmar, Olimpia Coral Melo Cruz whose activism got Mexico to pass a law prohibiting revenge porn, and Phyllis Omido, who fought for a $12 million settlement for lead-poisoning victims in her community in Kenya. Solidarity!

#Litigation.

If companies or governments won't go far enough, fast enough on climate action, perhaps it's time to use the law against them. We should never expect those who benefit from the status quo to take a lead in changing it. Today, this is especially true for the fossil fuel industry. The stick is needed as much as the carrot. The work of the Dutch attorney Roger Cox is a sign of things to come. In 2021, he took Royal Dutch Shell to court and secured a legal ruling that the company must reduce its emissions by 45% by 2030.

#CarbonLaw.

For COP-26 to succeed, it needs to embrace the Carbon Law for climate change. You've probably heard of Moore's Law for computing – the rule of thumb that computing power doubles every two years; maybe even Swanson's Law, where the price of solar panels tends to drop 20 percent for every doubling of installed capacity. The Carbon Law, proposed by a team of scientists led by Johan Rockström (of planetary boundaries fame), states that carbon emissions have to halve each decade to keep global warming within 1.5 degrees. With emissions still rising in 2021, the great U-turn cannot wait anymore.

#Billionaires.

There are 2,755 billionaires in the world with a collective net worth of $13.1 trillion. Besides the gross income inequality, it's worth asking how they use their wealth. Is it trips to space – which have overtaken private jets and luxury yachts as the latest status symbol – or something more meaningful? Outside of Brazil, how many people have even heard of the media billionaire Luiza Trajano, let alone how she uses her power and resources to promote equity and inclusion in a patriarchal society? It's easy to paint billionaires as immoral, but let's not tar all with the same brush.

#Anxiety.

As COP26 draws to a close, climate anxiety among young people is reaching fever pitch. The Lancet climate change survey of 10,000 16-25-year-olds in 10 countries published in September 2021 finds that 59% are very or extremely worried, and more than 50% feel sad, anxious, angry, powerless, helpless, and guilty. What to do? First, those with power in companies and governments must up their ambition and take bold action. Second, we must show how actions by cities, business, finance and civil society are accelerating positive change in a powerful convergence that is creating a virtuous spiral of systemic transformation.

#Movement.

Do you feel hope or despair after COP26 in Glasgow? I choose hope, and here's why. The 1.5°C ambition remains clearly in focus, climate justice is on the table and the world agreed to reduce fossil fuels. There were also multi-stakeholder agreements on deforestation, methane, coal, fossil fuels, clean energy and finance. These are clear signals and actions that reinforce one another. That's how complex systems change, by creating virtuous cycles of positive feedback loops, accelerating transformation. We are not out of danger; far from it. But COP26 just turned decarbonisation from an elite sport into a global movement.

#STEM.

At a recent dialogue with CEOs, hosted by Antwerp Management School, we talked about gender disparity, especially the gender pay gap. According to Françoise Chombar, Chairwomen of semiconductor manufacturing company MELEXIS, one key strategy for closing this gap is to increase the number of women working in STEM (science, technology, engineering, and mathematics), since these jobs pay better. She cited some powerful EU research that found exposing school pupils and university students to STEM female role models for between 15 and 60 minutes increased the number of girls and young women pursuing STEM education by between 28% and 47%.

#Intelligence.

There are reasons to be cautious about artificial intelligence, big data and machine learning. They can codify prejudice, manipulate behaviour and take away decision making control from humans. But its potential for good is also immense. Gro Intelligence, founded by Sara Menker, is using these powerful new technologies to tackle the world's biggest challenges, most notably food security and climate change. The ability to help farmers, companies and governments to anticipate risks (like locust plagues, crop diseases or extreme weather) and spot opportunities (growing demand, rising prices, or improved yields) can save money and lives. That's intelligence worth having.

#Attribution.

Weather is a short term occurrence; climate change is a long term pattern. That's why scientists have been hesitant to claim that climate change has caused any particular weather-related event, whether it be hurricanes, droughts, floods or wildfires. Climate change makes these events more likely, but we can't say for sure that they are linked to global warming. That narrative is finally changing, thanks to the World Weather Attribution project led by Friederike Otto and Geert Jan van Oldenborgh. Their deep statistical analysis is able to rapidly conclude that certain weather events are "virtually impossible without human-caused climate change".

#mRNA.

While we like to dramatize scientific breakthroughs, science is marathon, not a sprint. Nowhere is this more evident today than in the mRNA (messenger RNA) based COVID-19 vaccines that are saving millions of lives. Bringing the therapeutic potential of mRNA to fruition at this pivotal moment in human history relied on three decades of research by biochemists like Katalin Kariko, now a senior vice president at BioNTech, which collaborated with Pfizer to develop their vaccine. In a world obsessed with quick fixes and easy gains, it is good to be reminded that advancing science and improving society requires persistence.

#OneTen.

We often talk about the gender gap, which remains unacceptably wide and critical to address. But there is another gap that gets less airtime, which is the opportunity gap for Black talent. It's a problem that coalition organisation OneTen is making its audacious mission to solve. Co-founded by Kenneth Frazier and Kenneth Chenault, former CEOs of American Express and Merck respectively and among the few Black leaders to have run Fortune 500 companies, OneTen aims to hire, promote and advance one million Black Americans who do not have a four-year degree into family-sustaining careers over the next 10 years.

#Martian.

I like Matt Damon as the astronaut Mark Watney in Ridley Scott's film adaptation of 'The Martian' by Alex Weir. But as is often the case, the book is far more powerful. Weir is one of the world's most skilful living science fiction writers. But he has also unwittingly written one of the best case studies you'll ever read on entrepreneurship, resilience and the circular economy. The fact that it's fiction – grounded in science-based research – takes nothing away from the lessons and inspiration on offer about resource scarcity, creative adaptation and closing the loop on energy and material flows.

#Fruit.

We often think of biodiversity in terms of animals, but let's not forget diversity of plants, and especially food. If we celebrate and embrace food diversity, such as local varieties of fruits, vegetables and grains, we are supporting biodiversity with all its ecological benefits. One person who is taking this challenge to heart is Pablo Salvatierra, who experimented with a fruitarian diet when he was a 23-year-old Argentinian student struggling with a severe case of a skin disease called psoriasis. It seemed to help and now he is travelling the world sampling diverse fruits, more than 300 and counting.

#Welfare.

When it comes to animal welfare, we are still in the stone age. Campaigns like 'End the Cage Age' give us a clue about how little progress we have made, especially in industrial agriculture, where animals are treated as factors of production rather than sentient beings. It's not only cruelty-free farming – and plant-based or cultured meat alternatives – that can make a difference. Volvo has taken an ethical stand for animal welfare by going completely leather-free in future electric cars. Likewise, the fashion and textiles industries can choose cruelty-free practices by banning fur and choosing responsible down and vegan leathers.

#Commodities.

It's long been known that deforestation is strongly linked to unsustainable agricultural practices for food commodities like beef, wood, palm oil, soy, coffee and cocoa. At COP26, more than 100 countries representing 85% of the world's forests joined an agreement to halt and reverse deforestation by 2030. Sceptics pointed out that a similar 2014 agreement did not meet its targets. However, we already see the EU taking bold steps to turn talk into action, with a legal proposal to ban imports of these food commodities if their producers cannot prove that they resulted in no deforestation. Action beyond bla-bla-bla.

#Congo.

Do you associate the Congo in Africa with war, poverty, human displacement, corruption, and conflict minerals? You're not wrong, but you're missing something big. The Congo Basin rainforest, like the Amazon, is one of the world's lungs, absorbing 600 million tons of CO_2 a year (a third of US transportation emissions). The forest has given sanctuary to humans for 50,000 years and today 75 million people depend on it for survival, as do 10,000 species of plant, 1,000 species of birds, 700 species of fish and 400 species of mammals. And like the Amazon, it needs protection and restoration.

#Bioregions.

Maps can be misleading, especially when we want to understand the natural systems on which our lives depend. Most maps are either political, or infrastructural or geophysical. As a result, they don't tell us how nature is working together in pockets of symbiosis. Scientists call these bioregions, of which there are 185 in the world today. Bioregions cross political borders and physical geographies, each containing a limited number of ecoregions, totalling 844 on land and 62 in the oceans. This understanding emerges from relatively new science, giving us a fascinating, vital perspective on our place in the living world.

#Coastal.

How well are the world's economies prioritising the protection of ocean health, through sustainable marine activity, blue innovation, and policy implementation? The MIT Blue Technology Barometer ranks 66 coastal countries and territories on advancing ocean sustainability. The overall leaders are UK, Germany, Denmark, US, and Finland. There are also category leaders on protecting the ocean (Australia, Costa Rica, Canada), marine activity (Dominican Republic, UAE, Ecuador), technology innovation (China, South Korea, France) or policy and regulation (Belgium, Sweden, Ireland). The oceans give us life, livelihood and climate stabilisation. Viva la blue revolution!

#Decomposition.

Every year, we buy 100 billion garments. In Europe, fashion consumption has gone up 40% in the past 25 years, with 87% going to landfill or incineration. In addition, a third of microplastic pollution comes from clothing (two-thirds of all clothes use plastic fibres like polyester, nylon, acrylic, fleece and spandex). Calling for more circular fashion will only get us so far. We also have to rethink clothing materials – more especially if they are biodegradable. The Biomimicry Institute just won a €2.5 million grant to test and pilot technologies that convert wasted clothes and textiles into biocompatible raw materials.

#Tutu.

When I was growing up in South Africa and living through its transition to democracy, Desmond Tutu was the voice of morality that helped to banish apartheid and give birth to the 'rainbow nation', a term he coined to celebrate the diverse cultures in South Africa. When Mandela's government came to power, Tutu led the painful Truth and Reconciliation Commission, which helped the country confront its shadow past, grieve its losses and start to heal. Later, as a member of The Elders, his compassion, wisdom and humour shone brightly. He was a leader who embodied thriving. RIP Desmond Tutu.

#Wilson.

I discovered the brilliant work of Edward O. Wilson rather late in my sustainability career. But he was impossible to ignore. As a biologist and writer, he inspired a generation of ecological scientists and helped us to understand how living systems self-organise and thrive. One of his legacy gifts was 'biophilia', the scientific hypothesis that humans possess an innate tendency to seek connections with nature and other forms of life. He also left us with the Half-Earth challenge, to set aside 50% of land and sea for the 8.7 million other species that share our home. RIP E.O. Wilson.

#Future.

Kim Stanley Robinson's prescient science fiction novel 'The Ministry for the Future' gives some vital clues about how our global response to climate change may unfold in the coming decades. First, it will likely be messy; two-steps forward, one-step back, with many defeats and victories along the way. Second, it will almost certainly be a fight; make no mistake, this is a battle against powerful vested interests. And third, it can still end well; there is every reason to believe that we can turn things around through a combination of citizen action, policy reform, technology innovation and business transformation.

#iRepair.

In one of the biggest corporate policy U-turns in history, in 2022 Apple will start making parts and repair manuals available to individual customers. This is a huge win for circular economy advocates in the electronics sector, and is a tribute to the entrepreneurial gumption of modular design pioneers like Fairphone and Framework, and the tireless efforts of self-repair platforms like iFixit. The EU's right-to-repair legislation must take some credit as well. Apple will start selling parts and tools for the iPhone 12 and 13 in a Self Service Repair Online Store, along with service manuals and repair-enabling software.

#Virgin.

The good news is that "peak virgin plastic" appears to have been achieved by the 130 signatories of the Ellen MacArthur Foundation's circular economy for plastics Global Commitment, with predictions that it will fall 20% by 2025 against a 2018 baseline. The bad news is that less than 2% of signatories' plastic packaging is reusable, and for more than half of all signatories, this is 0%. The problem is that petrochemical companies – and by implication, we as customers – are not paying the full societal and environmental cost of virgin plastic. The time for a carbon tax is long overdue.

#Mushrooms.

Have you read 'Entangled Life' by Merlin Sheldrake, about 'how fungi make our worlds, change our minds, and shape our futures'? It is above all else a scientific treatise, but I especially liked the chapter on 'Radical Mycology', which talks about mycoremediation – how mushrooms can digest everything from chemical pesticides and plastic to oil spills and even cigarette butts. More positively, mycofabrication uses mycelium to grow alternatives to leather, packaging, skin, bricks, furniture and graphite, to mention but a few innovative applications. Ecovative is a pioneer in this space, working with the likes of Stella McCartney and IKEA.

#Reverence.

There is a remarkable open letter to the Presidents of the nine Amazonian countries, written by Nemonte Nenquimo, a leader of the Waorani people who live in the Amazon rainforest. The letter reveals the deeply sustainable worldviews of Indigenous communities. She reflects on the "thousands and thousands of years of love for this forest … Love in the deepest sense, as reverence. This forest has taught us how to walk lightly, and because we have listened, learned and defended her, she has given us everything: water, clean air, nourishment, shelter, medicines, happiness, meaning." `Now we should listen and learn.

#COVAX.

At the start of 2022, more than nine billion doses of coronavirus vaccines had been administered in 197 countries, but still only 50% of the global population is fully vaccinated. The global spike in Omicron cases is showing that no one is safe until everyone is safe. The COVAX program, which aims to ensure more equitable access, has shipped almost a billion vaccines, but the challenge remains colossal. Now a new, unpatented vaccine called CORBEVAX, using recombinant protein-based technology which is cheaper and more scalable in production, is set to launch, first in India with other countries to follow.

#Easy.

To create a thriving future, we need to make net positive choices easy. That means convenient and with no additional cost burden. A great example is BlocPower™, which has brought clean energy solutions to over 1,200 buildings low-income communities of American cities. What makes it easy? There is no upfront investment or loan and the cost of the upgrades are covered by regular payments are made out the customer's savings in energy utility bills (typically 20-40%). We need to apply a similar approach to other areas where there is a social, environmental and economic dividend over time.

#Monkeys.

Is your supply chain monkey-free? This may sound like a joke, but it's a serious question, at least for coconut farmers, where the exploitation of monkeys to retrieve the fruit is still commonplace. To tackle the issue, Thailand-based Theppadungporn Coconut Company has created the first audit scheme specifically designed to uncover monkey labor. This may seem like a very niche problem in a niche market, but it is a flag of more widespread and more serious animal abuse. Every year, up to 50,000 monkeys – mainly macaques and marmosets – are still used in research and testing human medicines and vaccines.

#Thriving.

It's time to move beyond sustainability (enduring, while doing less harm) to thriving (having a net positive impact). Why, you might ask, since we are not even sustainable yet? The reason is that the goal will determine the outcome. Right now, most sustainability efforts lack the ambition needed to match the scale and urgency of the problems. Extractive economies are growing; consumptive lifestyles are booming. Unless we aim for nature regeneration, flourishing societies and prosperous economies, we are planning to fail. Thriving is more inspiring – but also necessary to hold business and governments accountable for making a positive difference.

www.ingramcontent.com/pod-product-compliance
Lightning Source LLC
Chambersburg PA
CBHW061949070426
42450CB00007BA/1104